SALES TAX FOR AMAZON SELLERS

Expert Sales Tax Advice for Retailers Who

Sell on Internet Marketplaces

BY

Tim Nelson, CPA

Table of Contents

Introduction

With the rising popularity of e-commerce platforms like Amazon, eBay, and Etsy, small business owners and individuals looking to make supplemental income are increasingly turning to the internet as a place to make money. Understanding the sales tax implications of selling products online can be complicated at times, especially as states are trying to catch up on taxing e-commerce as a way to make up for revenue lost from declining sales at traditional brick and mortar stores. This book will provide an overview of how sales tax laws generally work, how to determine when sales tax is owed, and how recent changes to the law impact online merchants. After providing a big-picture discussion, the book will transition into more nuanced areas of the law, which may or may not apply to you and your business. The book will then discuss the cost of compliance and what can happen when a business is not fully compliant with the relevant tax laws. The book concludes with a few practical discussions aimed at helping ensure that you and your business avoid as many sales tax pitfalls as possible as you navigate through the realm of being a business owner. At the end of the book, you will find an appendix with helpful resources, including contact information for state revenue authorities tasked with overseeing the administration of sales taxes, some information about sales taxes that your business may be responsible for, a glossary, and a list of references. The list of references may be useful to you if you are looking for additional reading material.

The information contained in this book outlines a broad overview of issues related to sales tax. Laws related to sales tax issues can change at any time; some of the detailed information in this book—especially in the appendix—may be different several months or years down the road. As a business owner, you should ensure that you are aware of and complying with the laws as they are currently written and enforced. Some of the topics in this book address legal issues. This book should not be interpreted as offering legal advice in any way. This book provides a broad overview of the issues, and there may be specific issues that warrant a different approach than what is discussed in this book. You should consult with a tax attorney and/or a certified public accountant (CPA) who is familiar with the specific circumstances of your business in order to ensure that you are conducting your business in accordance with all applicable laws.

I hope you will enjoy this book, and I wish you the best of luck in your career as the owner of an online business. If you have any questions, please feel free to reach out to me. You can find out more information about me or contact me at my website, www.ebizaccounting.com, or reach me via phone at (914) 664-1900.

—Tim Nelson, CPA

1
When Must a Business Pay Sales Tax?

Historically, in states that collected sales tax, whether a business was required to collect and pay sales tax was based on whether that business had necessary nexus with the state. The nexus standard was established in the 1967 Supreme Court case of *National Bellas Hess, Inc. v. Department of Revenue of the State of Illinois* and modified slightly by the Court in *Quill Corp. v. North Dakota* in 1992. The *Quill* case established that the requisite nexus exists where a business has a sufficient physical presence in the state.

A business could establish a substantial nexus through three ways: (1) having an office in the state, (2) having an employee or making sales in the state, or (3) maintaining a warehouse or inventory storage facility in the state. Under the traditional nexus rule, an Amazon seller or merchant who utilized the Fulfilment by Amazon (FBA) service had substantial nexus in any state in which the merchant's inventory was stored.

2
What Has Changed?

With the increasing popularity of e-commerce over traditional brick-and-mortar stores, states began to look for ways to collect tax revenue from out-of-state internet retailers. Although every state that imposes a sales tax also imposes a use tax, usually at the same rate as the state's sales tax, states were still losing out on tax revenue they would have received if purchases had been made in physical stores instead of on the internet. A use tax is levied on items purchased out of state that will be used, stored, or consumed in the state where the consumer resides and on which no tax was collected when purchased. While the burden of collecting and remitting sales tax is placed on retailers, consumers are directly responsible for reporting and paying any use tax they may owe; because use tax payment is essentially on the honor system, compliance is extremely low, and it is estimated that only 2% of taxpayers actually report and pay the use tax that they owe.

Not only does the use tax–sales tax disparity result in a significant loss of tax revenue for states; it also gives internet retailers an edge over brick-and-mortar retailers. For example, if an out-of-state internet retailer and a physical store are both selling an identical widget for $100, most consumers would opt to buy from the internet retailer. Why? Because the grand total for the widget purchased online would still be $100, as no sales tax would be due; on the other hand, the physical store would be obligated to charge sales tax, so the grand total would be over $100. Of course, the consumer purchasing the widget online would still technically be obligated to pay the state's use tax, but as indicated above, most consumers fail to do so.

Legal scholars also began to question the prudence of the traditional *Quill* rule. In 2015 the Supreme Court began to show signs that some justices were willing to revisit the issue in *Quill*, and states began passing "kill *Quill*" legislation designed to trigger a legal challenge and force the Supreme Court to revisit the issue. One such state was South Dakota, which enacted a law that would impose sales tax on out-of-state retailers who had an economic nexus with the state. The statute required out-of-state retailers to collect and pay sales tax if they had annual sales over $100,000 or made at least 200 transactions with South Dakota residents in a year.

Eventually more than 20 states passed similar "kill *Quill*" legislation. In essence, what these states were telling retailers was, "If you have over a certain amount of sales in a state, you now have a sufficient nexus with us, and we are going to impose our sales tax on you because of this." With the increasing popularity of companies like Amazon, states could now take advantage of sales to their residents that they could not tax under the *Quill* rule. Take Rhode Island for example, which does not currently have an Amazon Fulfilment Center. Rhode Island could pass legislation that requires out-of-state retailers with an economic nexus to collect and remit sales tax. Any out-of-state retailer that has a certain amount of sales would have a nexus with the state and would have to file tax returns and collect and remit taxes. Under such legislation Rhode Island would be generating a significant amount of additional revenue that was previously inaccessible.

3
Paying Sales Tax for Amazon Sales

As a merchant, you are ultimately responsible for ensuring that you are complying with states' sales tax laws, so the responsibility of collecting and paying sales tax is on you. That being said, there are currently two states for which Amazon automatically calculates, collects, and remits sales tax for orders shipped to those states on behalf of third-party merchants. Amazon does this because both Washington and Pennsylvania have passed laws requiring all online marketplaces to collect and remit sales tax on behalf of their third-party sellers. Even if Amazon pays your sales tax, you will still need to file a sales tax return if you have a sales tax permit with the state.

4
Calculating Sales Tax Owed

Amazon collects all the data regarding your sales and how much sales tax they have collected for you. You can review and download all of this information directly from your Amazon Seller Central portal. Another method for tracking sales tax information is to use software or an application that works with the data supplied by Amazon. A popular example of such an application is TaxJar, which has the capability of setting up integration with Amazon and a number of other marketplace websites. Another company providing a range of tax compliance products for businesses is Avalara. These integrated applications pull out all of the sales and sales tax data provided by Amazon for each filing period and produce a report telling you how much you have to pay in sales tax to each state. Most products have the capability of also breaking down sales at the county or city level for areas where a local sales tax is also collected, and some applications even allow you to set up automated tax return filing—although this usually has an additional cost.

A number of factors can affect which software or application might be right for you, including your total sales, states in which you sell, how automated or hands-on you want the application to be, and your budget. More information about TaxJar can be found at www.taxjar.com, and more information about Avalara can be found at www.avalara.com. Although TaxJar and Avalara are two of the more popular tax compliance companies, you should do your own research to see what software or application best fits your needs.

5

Determining Nexus with States

The number of states with which you have a nexus requiring you to pay sales tax will vary based on a number of factors. At times making this determination can be somewhat complicated. One easy determination is whether you owe sales tax to your home state. Wherever you live or are operating your business out of, you automatically have nexus there because you are the owner of your business. Therefore, you would have nexus with that state. Unless you live in one of the few states without a sales tax, you will be responsible for paying sales tax in your home state; even if you live in a state without a sales tax, you may be responsible for sales tax levied at the local level. For a list of sales tax rates by state and a list of which states permit local governments to levy sales tax, see the Appendix.

Other states in which you would have nexus are the states in which Amazon is storing your inventory in a FBA warehouse. There are currently over 30 states with Amazon Fulfillment Centers, and the number of states with a fulfillment center is likely to continue to rise. Amazon also has a number of "sort centers" spread out throughout the country, and it is important to differentiate between fulfillment centers and sort centers because product moving through a sort center alone does not create a sufficient nexus with that state for sales tax purposes.

Finally, as discussed in Chapter 2, merchants can be obligated to pay sales tax in states where they have a sufficient economic nexus.

Most, but not all, states that levy a sales and/or use tax have enacted an economic nexus law; given the Supreme Court's decision in *Wayfair*, it is likely that those states who have not yet done so will probably do so in the future. While the broad theory behind economic nexus laws is essentially the same from state to state, there is some significant variation in the threshold states have set in their economic nexus laws. Some states have set a threshold based on gross revenue in the state alone, while others have set a threshold based on gross revenue or total sales in the state. A small minority of states has set the threshold based on both gross revenue and total sales in the state. A list of threshold by state can be found in the Appendix. Because of the recent nature of the *Wayfair* decision, this is an area of tax law that has the potential to remain somewhat volatile for the foreseeable future.

6

Determining States Where Amazon Is Storing Inventory

You can view and download a report of where your inventory has been stored through your Seller Central portal. There are a number of Amazon Fulfillment reports available to merchants, including an Inventory Event Detail report. This report allows you to see all of the fulfillment centers where your inventory has been stored for a given period of time. The fulfillment centers are labelled according to the closest airport with a number after the airport code to differentiate between multiple centers near that airport. For example, "BOS1" would refer to a fulfillment center near Boston, Massachusetts, while "CHA1" and "CHA2" would refer to two different fulfillment centers both near Chattanooga, Tennessee. A list of airport codes can easily be found on the internet.

Determining nexus based on inventory location can be complicated at times. With the rising popularity of Amazon Prime, Amazon has put a lot of focus on making sure that deliveries are made on time. As a result, Amazon wants to spread out and relocate your inventory, so it is important to stay up-to-date on where your products are being stored. Additionally, it is important to realize that your inventory may be moved from the original Amazon center to which you send your items. This is especially relevant for merchants utilizing Amazon's Inventory Placement Service. The Inventory Placement Service is a program designed to make the shipment process easier for merchants;

instead of having shipments divided into multiple shipments, merchants who use Inventory Placement Service have the ability to send all of their eligible inventory items to a single center for a per-item fee. Amazon then splits up the inventory to different fulfillment centers. A misconception some merchants have is that they can utilize the Inventory Placement Service to keep limit their nexus to one state; however, nexus is not simply determined by where inventory is initially sent but also where it is stored. Additionally, even those using Amazon's standard shipping plan should be aware that Amazon chooses the center to which a merchant's inventory should be sent, and this can change from shipment to shipment.

7

Registering in States Where You Have Nexus

The next step after determining where you have nexus and sales—or are likely to have nexus and sales in the near future—is to register for a sales tax license. Assuming that you plan on selling your products in your home state, you should register for a sales tax license in your home state—ideally even before you make your first sale. After this, the decision is ultimately up to you when to register in states where you may have nexus based on inventory or economic nexus. When it comes to nexus based on inventory storage, the conservative approach for merchants utilizing FBA is to register in every state where Amazon has a fulfillment center. While this will help guarantee that you are complying with all relevant tax laws, it may be unnecessary and cause pointless work for you. Depending on the nature of your business, there may be states with fulfillment centers where your product will never be stored and/or shipped to; as a result, you may end up collecting and/or filing unnecessarily. Many states require you to file a sales tax return once you register for a license, even if it means simply filing a zero sales tax return; the consequences for not filing could be a penalty even if the underlying amount you owe is nothing. Therefore, unnecessarily registering for a license where you have no nexus and/or sales could create extra administrative work. If you do decide to take the conservative approach, make sure that you comply with states' filing requirements so that you avoid getting hit with a penalty. Also, most states make it illegal to collect sales tax without a

12

license, so make sure that if you are collecting sales tax from purchasers in a state that you have the permit to do so.

At the point that you choose to register for a sales tax license in each state, basically all you have to do is go to the Department of Revenue (or similar equivalent) website for each state and register your company in that state for a sales tax license. Each state's website will walk you through how to register for a sales tax permit. The websites will also notify you about basic information such as how often you have to file a sales tax return; this could be monthly, quarterly, or annually. Most states' websites will also let you know that you also need to file income taxes on top of any sales taxes that are due. Having nexus in a state usually means that you will have both sales tax responsibilities and income tax responsibilities. Income tax laws will vary from state to state, and there may also be other applicable taxes. Some states charge a "franchise tax" on businesses (which will be discussed in Chapter 10), while others charge a "gross receipts tax" instead of an income tax, taxing your gross receipts instead of profits.

Before you register, you will want to gather all of the necessary documents. Each state will differ in what they require you to provide at the time of registering, but the following is a general list of what some states may require:

- Address

- Social Security Number

- Driver's License Number or State Identification

- Business entity type

- Federal Employee Identification Number (FEIN)

- State Identification Number

- Information about your business activity

- Banking information

- Incorporation documents

Again, each state will differ in what is required. It is best to check with the state where you want to register to see what specifically they will require of you. For a full list of resources and contact information related to registering for sales tax licenses, see the Appendix.

8
Businesses Located Outside of the United States

All sellers, even international sellers located outside of the United States, have to follow the exact same tax rules as if they were located in the U.S. This means that international merchants form nexus with states in the same way American merchants do and still have to register for sales tax in the same way that American merchants have to. This applies to merchants and sellers based in any country across the globe.

Once an international merchant starts doing business in the United States, the same tax laws that apply to American merchants are immediately applicable. If you are an international merchant utilizing FBA, this means that you will likely have nexus in every state with a fulfillment center, assuming that Amazon spreads out your inventory. Similarly, the economic nexus rules allowed under *Wayfair* are applicable to international merchants.

One important thing to note regarding international merchants is that, in general, tax treaties between the U.S. and a foreign government are irrelevant when it comes to sales tax. Because states are not parties to these treaties and because sales taxes are set at the state or local level, states are not bound by—and most do not recognize—such tax treaties. This means that an internationally based merchant who is not subject to federal taxes can be responsible for state and local taxes.

9
"Amazon Laws"

There are two other forms of nexus that states have established that fall under the broader category of what some have labelled "Amazon laws"—laws states have crafted in order to tax internet sales. Two types of nexus states have established through these "Amazon laws" are click-through nexus and affiliate nexus. Although they are closely related, there are distinctions, and it is important to understand these distinctions, as states may have laws regarding click-through nexus, affiliate nexus, or both.

Click-through nexus laws establish that out-of-state merchants who contract with individuals or companies in the state to refer customers to the merchant through a web link for a commission or other compensation is considered to have nexus with that state. In general, payments for pay-per-click and banner advertisements do not establish click-through nexus unless the payment is contingent upon a sale. Most states establish a threshold of referred sales that a merchant must exceed before the merchant is presumed to have nexus with the state. Some states have "rebuttable presumption" laws, allowing merchants to show that the in-state individuals or companies with which they have agreements did not engage in solicitation on behalf of the merchant. Other states have "irrebuttable presumption" laws, meaning that a merchant has no way of administratively challenging the state's decision that click-through-nexus has been established.

Consider the following example to understand when click-through nexus exists and does not exist. Assume that you have a company based in Michigan that sells widgets on Amazon; you have a number of different widgets that you sell, so you set up an Amazon Store with a customized design and unique URL so that you can promote your widgets. You heard from a friend that she had success promoting her products through Facebook advertising, so you decide to set up an ad campaign on Facebook. With Facebook advertising, you have to pay regardless of whether your ad campaign generates a single sale, so this would not qualify as click-through nexus, regardless of how much you make as a result of the advertising campaign—the payments for the advertising are not at all contingent on a sale being made. As your business continues to grow, you are looking for more opportunities to promote your widgets, so you decide to attend a widget and gadget convention; at the convention, you meet a gadget seller based in Tennessee who thinks that customers who buy his gadgets might also be interested in buying your widgets. He agrees to link to your Amazon Store on his website for a 5% commission of any sales made, and the results are a huge success for you; hundreds of people found your Amazon Store through the gadget website and purchased your widgets—resulting in $20,000 worth of sales. This would qualify as click-through nexus.

Similar to click-through nexus is affiliate nexus; affiliate nexus laws establish that an out-of-state seller is deemed to have nexus with a state if the merchant uses an in-state individual or business for services related to the merchant's sales. For example, if an out-of-state merchant has an agreement with an in-state service provider to provide repairs or maintenance on the merchant's products, this would qualify as affiliate nexus. Affiliate nexus also applies to services related to storage and warehouse maintenance.

For Amazon sellers, apart from affiliate nexus through FBA warehouses, click-through nexus laws are likely to be more applicable than affiliate nexus laws. A list of states with click-through nexus laws and their thresholds can be found in the Appendix. Keep in mind that these laws can change, and more states are likely to adopt click-through nexus and/or affiliate nexus laws to take advantage of the increasing popularity of e-commerce over brick and mortar stores. Application of these laws to individual merchants can be complex at times, and it may be beneficial to talk to a tax professional to determine what impact these "Amazon laws" may have on your business.

10
Nexus and State Income Tax

In 1959 the Supreme Court, in the case of *Northwestern Cement Co v. Minnesota*, ruled that a state could impose an income tax on a foreign corporation that leased office space in Minnesota for its sales representatives. The *Northwestern Cement* ruling created unintended consequences, and all of a sudden, businesses that produced products in a single location had to determine how their income needed to be divided among multiple jurisdictions where they had nexus. Congress reacted by passing the Interstate Income Act of 1959 (also referred to as Public Law 86-272). That law protected businesses with only minimal contacts with a state from being liable for state income taxes; under Public Law 86-272, a business can solicit sales of personal property though creating a nexus for state income tax purposes. Anything beyond soliciting sales of personal property (and a few actions closely related to such solicitation) would create a nexus for income tax purposes. For example, selling or providing services, accepting orders, delivering property, and storing inventory in a state would all create a nexus for income tax purposes.

As discussed previously, with the increase of e-commerce, states have felt like they are losing out on potential revenue, so some states have turned to income tax as a means of making up this lost revenue. What some states have said is if a company has nexus with the state, that company is obligated to pay income tax to the state and file an income tax return. Unlike transactional taxes (sales tax and use tax) taxes on business activities, like income tax, franchise tax, and gross

19

receipts tax, were not limited by the traditional *Bellas Hess* and *Quill* rules that required a physical presence to create a nexus. Even before the *Wayfair* decision, states could use economic nexus as a means of subjecting businesses to income tax (and other business activities taxes).

Many states will collect fees that you will owe for income taxes, whether you are just a sole proprietor or if you are a limited liability company (LLC), a corporation, an S corporation, or a partnership. States can charges a fee for doing business in the that state, and those fees vary. This is a way that the states increase their revenue and increase your reporting responsibilities in each state so that they get their money. Many Amazon sellers and other internet merchants do not realize that they have to register and file tax returns because of their nexus in each state; to be fully compliant, you may have to file both a sales tax return and an income tax return for each state where you have a sufficient nexus.

11
Franchise Taxes

As an alternative to income taxes, many states also impose franchise taxes, which are usually based on a business's capital or net worth; franchise taxes are usually owed annually. A franchise tax will usually be applicable if you are not required to file any income taxes in the state or if the amount you owe under the franchise tax would be greater than what you would owe under the income tax. For example, if you are an S corporation and you do not owe any tax on your income, the state may still charge a franchise fee.

A perfect example of this is California. California—no matter what your revenue is—will charge you a franchise fee for registering your business in California because you have nexus. California has a sales tax and a corporate income tax. Additionally, the state has a $800 minimum franchise tax applicable to S corporations, LLCs, limited partnerships (LPs), limited liability partnerships (LLPs), and corporations that are not subject to the general corporate income tax. So just to do business in the state of California, you have to pay $800 to the Franchise Tax Board in the state of California every year. Once you start making money and start showing profits in the state of California, the amount due under the franchise tax increases. Under California's franchise tax, the amount you owe will be a flat amount based on which income bracket your business falls under, and this tax will be owed just for doing business in California.

There are currently 15 states that impose a franchise tax. Some states impose both a corporate income tax and a franchise tax, while others only impose one or the other. Although not every state imposes $800 for their franchise tax, if you are registered in a lot of states, this can quickly add up. Keep in mind that if you are utilizing FBA, you likely have nexus with at least 30 states, so you could owe franchise taxes to several states just to have the ability to do business in those states.

12
The Cost of Compliance

The biggest thing that people do not realize is what the total cost of compliance is. Essentially, your cost of compliance is the total amount that it costs you as a seller to comply with each state's tax laws so that you do not have any problems with any state regulatory authorities, the IRS, etc. One of the important questions that has likely come into your mind as you read this book has been what the cost of compliance will be to you and your business.

First you have to make sure you file all your sales tax returns on time. For the sake of this example, assume that you have inventory in all 30 states where Amazon currently has a FBA warehouse and that you are also based in one of those states. That means that in order to be fully compliant, you would have registered in 30 states to file and pay sales tax. Because this would be incredibly burdensome to calculate all on your own, you use software or an application online that charges you $30 per month, and you have to file every month. If you file every month and the average fee is $30 per filing, your costs for simply filing sales tax add up pretty quickly: $30 × 30 states × 12 months = $10,800. So right off the bat, just to be compliant you have to pay $10,800 to somebody just to file your sales tax returns for you. Keep in mind that this is unrelated to anything that is actually bringing money into your business; this is simply one of the costs of being compliant.

Next you have to file income tax returns. Whether your business is formed as a corporation, an LLC, or a partnership—or even if you are filing a personal return as a sole proprietor—you again need to file a state income tax return with 30 different states. Microsoft does not file a 30-state tax return. Apple does not file a 30-state tax return. But you, the Amazon seller, as small as you are or as large as you are, have to file a 30-state income tax return breaking down how much revenue was sold in all those states. If you were to go to any accountant or a certified public accountant (CPA) and say, "Hi, I need a return filed with 30 states," odds are that person is going to turn around say, "Alright, that is going to be about $65,000." That is actually probably pretty close to the amount that you would be charged by a CPA to file that many income tax returns. And so you may turn around and say, "Wait, I have to pay $10,800 for sales tax plus $65,000 to a tax preparer, a CPA, or an accountant—and there is a difference between each one—to file my tax returns? That's over $75,000!" You're right! That is why the rules, as they currently are, are just not fair. But this is the actual cost of compliance. That is how far you would be behind the eight ball. Think about how difficult it would be for you to start in this business and succeed when you are already in the red more than $75,000. How are you supposed to make money? Hopefully you have a product in place and are making a profit—at least so that you can cover the cost of compliance.

13
Other Options to Ensuring Compliance

Having seen the cost of compliance in the last chapter, you may be thinking that your only option is to hire a full-time accountant, but this is not the case. Fortunately, there are other options for you and your business.

What some people do—and this is something that states are cracking down on—is to only register in states where they are making a significant amount of sales. For example, if you have a new business that is just starting out and you want to start selling on Amazon, you probably cannot afford the fees associated with being registered in 30 states. You are a small business, and you are not on anybody's radar yet. In this situation, what you should start off doing is first registering in your home state. When you start your business, whether you are selling as a sole proprietor or are actually forming an entity such as a partnership, an LLC, or a corporation, you need to register for a sales tax in your license. Assuming that you actually make a sale, there is no way around this; you will owe sales tax and have to file sales tax and income tax returns in your home state.

Beyond your home state, no other state in the country has any idea who you are. There is no list they can look at, and there is nothing they can look up. When you are starting off, only the state you live in knows who you are or what the name of your business is.

So when you are just starting out, you collect sales tax on Amazon by setting up your Amazon seller account to only collect sales tax for sales in your home state; you file your sales tax returns, and you file your income tax return at the end of the year. That is pretty much the minimal tax compliance cost you could possibly have.

After a while your business starts growing—everybody loves your product. Your sales are starting to grow, and you are starting to make larger profits. You may want to take a more conservative approach in order to cover yourself. You begin to realize that it is not a great idea to just be registered in your home state, and you are worried about other states coming after you—and rightfully so. What you should do now is analyze all of your sales and determine the states in which you are making the most sales. For example, you know that Texas, California, New York, and Washington are the states that have your largest sales. As a result, those are the states where you have your largest potential liabilities. The best course of action is to just register in those states; you probably do not need to register in every state with which you have nexus. So instead of registering in dozens of additional states, you just register in an additional four.

At this point you have pretty much covered all the states from which you are generating the most revenue. For example, if your home state is Illinois and Kentucky, which has a sales tax rate of 6%, is one of the states that you are technically supposed to be registered in, it may cost you $2,500 a year to register and file returns—just to be compliant. Meanwhile, your sales in the state of Kentucky are only $800. From a financial standpoint, it just does not make sense to be registered in Kentucky. Think about it in terms of a cost–benefit analysis. What is the worst that could happen if you do not register in Kentucky and remit the required sales taxes? If the state of Kentucky finds out that you failed to remit the owed taxes, the state government will come to you saying, "Hey, you owe us! You had $800 worth of sales in our state, and you owe sales tax of $48." So in response, you will acknowledge that you owe the $48 and pay it—with probably a little extra in a penalty and interest. On the downside, you had to pay a little extra money in penalties and interest, but on the upside, you went years without having to pay $2,500 every year just to stay completely technically compliant.

As you start to grow, the best approach is to continually register in the states where you have a lot of sales. The number of states you are registered in over time will likely grow, but using this method will keep your overall cost of compliance as low as possible without putting your business at risk of getting hit with significant interest or penalties for unpaid sales tax obligations.

14

Responding to a Compliance Letter from a State

If you have been selling your product online for a while and you get a compliance letter from a state in which you have not filed, saying that you owe money for unpaid sales taxes, you need to make sure that you react to and respond to that letter appropriately. If you get a letter from a state saying that they believe you have nexus with them and owe them back sales tax, you should contact your certified public accountant to help with help on how to do this not your bookkeeper or somebody who just says he is an accountant but an actual CPA, because there is a chance that you do not actually owe anything.

States will manipulate and change your responses to be favorable to them. For example, think about what your answers would be to some simple hypothetical questions a state might ask you: "Do you have any inventory in our state?" If you respond by just saying, "Yes," but you only had inventory in the state for three days or three months, the state will turn that around and interpret your answer as meaning that you had inventory in the state for the entire three years for which they believe you owe back taxes. So they will assess the liability for the entire past three years, even though you may not have actually been obligated to pay sales tax for that long. This is a perfect example of why you do not want to just turn around respond to a letter like that without consulting with a professional.

You also do not want to just ignore it, even though you think that might be a viable option because the state trying to come after you still probably has no idea who you are. You may be thinking that they are just fishing for information—just sending the letter or questionnaire looking for you to respond so they have more information on you. In actuality, at the point that you are getting one of these letters in the mail, if you are on the state's radar for possibly owing back sales tax, the reality to them is that you are a "large business owner" to them. A state is not going to want to waste time going after smaller business, because the money simply is not there to go after small businesses. A state is going to spend far more money to send someone to audit a small business than the state would recover in any back taxes that might actually be owed. So the odds are that if you are getting a letter from a state saying, "Hey, we think you owe back sales tax and sales tax going forward," the letter should be taken seriously. Hopefully you already have a CPA you can consult with so that he or she can advise you and help guide you in the right direction on how to respond to the letter. If you do not have a CPA already lined up, it would be a good idea to find one to consult with.

15
Sales Tax Audits

Beyond simply sending compliance letters to ensure that merchants are complying with sales tax laws and regulations, states also conduct sales tax audits of businesses. The process if you get audited for sales taxes would be that an auditor would come to your place of business—or, hopefully if you have a CPA, the CPA would have the auditor come down to your CPA's office to perform the audit. During the audit the auditors will want to look at your sales numbers. They want to look at your revenue to determine two things: first, they will want to know what your sales are, and second, they will want to know if you actually have nexus with the state.

Sales tax auditors cannot just show up at your office and say, "You owe us this money." They first have to prove that you have nexus with the state, should be registered, and should be required to collect sales tax. In order to do this, the state will have to get information about what inventory you had in the state and when you had it there, and this is the state's burden. They may have to subpoena records from Amazon to show this. Before they can collect back sales tax from you, the auditors need to prove that you had inventory in a warehouse in the state for the requisite amount of time.

This is why it is important for you to not just immediately submit to their questioning and assume that you owe them back sales tax and have to pay the amount they are claiming you owe. It is important for you to work with your CPA and talk with the state and argue with what they are claiming, because they are still struggling to understand exactly how Amazon works. There are honestly a lot of employees at state departments of revenue who have no idea how it works. Meanwhile, instead of taking it slow and actually trying to figure out how it all works, states are just sending letters to as many people and businesses as possible with the hope that a portion of recipients will respond and unwittingly admit to their allegations that they have nexus with the state. When a business owner does this, the state can just turn around, make a quick assessment, and easily collect "their" money; the auditors never have to go through the trouble of proving that the business had nexus with the state.

Most states do not want to come out and audit every single person. By responding to or filling out the questionnaires, you are not putting the interests of you and your business first. Remember that most of the employees at these state departments of revenue do not understand how all the different types of inventory move around in Amazon and how the whole system works. Submitting to these types of audits is usually not the best option.

16

Inventory in a State Versus Sales in a State

Being located in a state, having inventory physically located in a state, or having economic nexus with a state is what places an obligation on you to have to file a sales tax return in that state—it is what gives you nexus with the state. However, your actual sales tax obligation, the amount you are required to collect and remit to the state, is based on your sales in the state over a given period of time.

As Amazon spreads your inventory to various fulfillment centers across the country, by doing so you are establishing the requisite nexus with each state where your inventory is stored, and that is what is giving you the obligation to file sales tax in that state. After determining which states you need to file sales tax returns in, the next step is to calculate the amount of sales tax you owe. Your sales in those states is how they calculate what your sales tax is. Amazon tracks your total sales, and if most of your sales are in states where there is no FBA warehouse, you may not have nexus with that state and therefore have no sales tax obligation with that state.

There are two big caveats to this general principle. The first is that you will always have nexus in any state where you, your employees, or your offices are physically located; therefore, you will have sales tax obligations to your home state(s). Second, if you are a more well-established business, you may have economic nexus with a state and will have sales tax obligations to those states now that the *Wayfair* case established that states can tax businesses based on economic nexus.

For the states where you have no nexus, everything is pretty easy. You simply do not have to collect sales tax and have no sales tax obligation. On the other hand, for states where you do have nexus and sales, you are required to collect and remit sales taxes to the state and file a sales tax return.

17
Worst-Case Scenario After an Audit

If you are audited and a state determines and proves that you do owe back sales tax, the worst-case scenario is that you will have to pay the money—probably with some penalties and interest. Depending on how large the sum is, you may be able to work out a payment plan. States will generally be willing to work with a business owner who is sincere about wanting to pay an amount owed in back sales tax. A state has little to gain in collecting a large lump sum from a business owner if it means bankrupting the business. Not only would this strategy risk the state not getting the entire amount it is owed, but it will result in the state generating no sales tax revenue as a result of that business going forward. By agreeing to a payment plan, the state can ensure that it gets the full amount it is owed while still allowing the business to make sales in the state—which brings in even more tax revenue over time.

18
Interest and Penalties

As mentioned in the previous chapter, you will likely be charged a penalty for not filing on time, and you may also owe some interest. If you are able to set up a payment plan to pay back the balance owed, you will have to pay interest as part of that payment plan. You will probably want to hire someone to negotiate with the state; although states typically cannot remove interest that has already accrued, the revenue agents may have the ability to work with you to decrease the penalty assessed. It is also in your best interest to file your returns on time even if you cannot pay the full amount at the time of filing; although interest will continue to accrue on the unpaid balance, filing in a timely manner may reduce your penalties. Making partial payments will also reduce the amount of interest you owe and may reduce the penalties assessed.

Although every situation is unique, if you get to the point where you are actually being audited, it may be worth it to hire a professional—probably a tax attorney—to represent you during the audit. A tax attorney will be able to negotiate a final number that the state is agreeable to that will hopefully be easier for you and your business to manage.

19
Voluntary Disclosure

States have quite a few different means of attempting to get e-commerce sellers to fully comply with their tax laws. One method is pushing voluntary disclosure—what they are essentially doing is using scare tactics to ensure compliance. There are frequently stories in the news about states cracking down on online merchants and finding sellers who owe astronomical amounts in back taxes. But before you start worrying about the latest headline about someone owing $1 million in back taxes, think about how much revenue someone needs to be generating to owe that much. If that merchant is selling in a state with a 7% sales tax, he would have sold over $14 million worth of his product to rack up $1 million in sales tax.

While you likely do not have to worry about owing $1 million in back taxes, if you realize that you have been noncompliant in a state and are worried about owing a significant chunk of change after an audit, a Voluntary Disclosure Agreement (VDA) may be a viable option for you. VDAs are binding agreements between a taxpayer and the state. In general, states will reduce or waive penalties for merchants entering into a VDA; VDAs typically limit the look-back period for which the merchant can be held liable for unpaid taxes. While every state is different, most states do not allow a business owner to enter into a VDA after the state has contacted the business about potential tax liability or an audit. VDAs are all about *voluntary* compliance; states have little interest in giving a huge break to someone who is only cooperating after getting caught failing to pay taxes.

While most VDA applications are fairly straightforward and simple, depending on your particular circumstances, it may be beneficial to have a tax professional assist you. In addition to assisting you during the application process, talking with a tax professional may also help you determine whether a VDA is right for you and your business.

20
Personal Liability for Your Business's Sales Tax

In general, one of the primary reasons people structure their companies as an LLC, a corporation, etc., is to avoid personal liability for any obligations the business owes and separate you personally from the business. (General partnerships and businesses run as sole proprietorships, however, do not shield owners from any liability.) If your online business is structured as an LLC and someone files a lawsuit against your business, they can go after the assets of the business, but you are generally personally protected (with some limited exceptions).

There are generally two types of business taxes for which individuals in a business can be personally liable for: payroll taxes and sales taxes. Many states have laws that say that a "responsible person" can be held liable for sales and payroll taxes owed by the business. While the definition of who is a responsible person can be somewhat complex—especially in larger companies—in general, someone with a significant ownership stake in a company or who is involved with the preparation of tax returns will qualify as a responsible person. Therefore, if you own your business or are responsible for preparing the tax returns, you will likely qualify as a responsible person.

As a practical matter, if a state discovers that your business owes back sales tax, their first step is not going to be to immediately ask you to personally pay the money owed. Typically states go after responsible parties as a last resort, such as when the business is insolvent.

21
Pass-Through Taxation

Sales tax is a type of "pass-through" tax because the money simply *passes* from the customer *through* the business and to the government. In theory, it is not supposed to cost the entity through which it passes anything, although as discussed in Chapter 12, the costs of compliance can be quite high. When done properly, a business will never have to actually "pay" any sales tax; the business will just collect and remit the proper amount of sales tax from its customers and to the government.

On the other hand, if a business collects sales tax but fails to then remit it to the state, instead spending it on something else, that is a problem. After all, that was never really the business's money to spend in the first place. If the state finds out that a business collected sales tax but did not pass it on to them, they will go after the business, because it was not the business's money to spend. If the business cannot come up with the money, this is where personal liability may come into play. Therefore, it is crucial to remember that whatever amount you are collecting in sales tax needs to be in turn paid to the state.

22

Mitigating a Business's Sales Tax Obligations

As indicated earlier, one of the methods of mitigating your sales tax obligation is to limit where you register to states where most of your sales happen or may happen. Some of those states will likely be Texas and California, as well as your home state. You will also likely want to register in Massachusetts, Pennsylvania, and Washington, due to laws and legal actions specific to those states.

In January 2018 Amazon began collecting sales tax on behalf of third-party sellers for sales in the state of Washington. This was done in response to Washington enacting a "marketplace facilitator law" requiring online marketplaces to collect sales taxes on behalf of anyone utilizing their platforms. Despite Amazon collecting sales tax on behalf of merchants, individual merchants are still required to file a Washington sales tax return if they have nexus with the state. Washington does have a FBA fulfillment center, so it is likely that you will have nexus with the state, but if you have no nexus with the state, you are not required to file a tax return.

In April 2018 Amazon began collecting sales tax on third-party sales in Pennsylvania in response to that state's marketplace facilitator law. With states looking for ways to recoup lost sales tax revenue in light of consumers increasingly switching from brick and mortar stores to e-commerce, it is likely that more states will enact marketplace facilitator laws. While these laws do not have a direct impact on a seller's nexus with a state—the laws do not actually change whether a merchant has nexus and do not require registration by merchants without nexus—they do raise the stakes for noncompliant merchants. Marketplace facilitator laws give states another tool to find noncompliant businesses and may place a merchant on the state's radar who otherwise would not be there. The state of Washington has been known for its aggressiveness when it comes to out-of-state merchants who owe back sales taxes; if its marketplace facilitator law is successful in increasing compliance, other states may follow suit.

Although Massachusetts does not (yet) have a marketplace facilitator law, the Massachusetts Department of Revenue sent a legal demand to Amazon in early 2018, requesting that Amazon turn over to the state information about merchants selling on Amazon, such as federal tax ID numbers and the value of merchants' inventory stored in FBA warehouses in the state. Massachusetts plans on using this information to identify businesses and individuals who should have been collecting and remitting sales tax but have failed to do so.

As more states pass similar laws, it is important for you as a merchant to keep up-to-date on developments similar to those in Washington, Pennsylvania, and Massachusetts. This can be a complicated task, so it may be beneficial for you to work with a tax professional to assist you. Apart from registering in states where you know you are likely to be on the government's radar, as discussed earlier, you should register in states where you have significant sales. Going back to the idea that sales taxes are pass-through taxes, it may not make sense to spend the $360 per year to be compliant in a state where your sales tax obligations are only $50; however, if your sales tax obligations to a state are hundreds or thousands of dollars a year, it is probably best to register.

You want to do what you can to make sure that your cost of compliance does not go through the roof. It is hard enough to start a new business, get it to grow, and actually make some money. The tax laws across the country are generally not favorable to e-commerce sellers—especially those on Amazon—because the cost of compliance is astronomically high. Registering in the states where you are physically located, where you have the highest sales, and where departments of revenue are specifically targeting internet retailers is the best way to keep your cost of compliance low while still not putting your business at risk of getting hit with unbearable penalties and interest.

23
Advocating for Simplifying the Tax Laws

Using the strategies discussed in this book may help to mitigate the burdens on your business, but mitigating these burdens is more akin to a bandage than a cure. At the root of the issue is that the tax schemes across the country are not friendly to e-commerce businesses—especially small businesses. There are groups out there who realize this and who are trying to organize to promote change. The Online Merchants Guild was recently formed by online merchants who are trying to organize more merchants to band together and lobby on behalf of sellers. Especially in the wake of things like Massachusetts completely skipping the legislative process and going directly to Amazon to hand over third-party seller information, there are a lot of online sellers who feel that their interests are not being adequately represented.

Right now the states are acting like the wild, wild west. They are making up any rule they can without any real checks or balances so that they can tax e-commerce sellers. Some of the laws and rules they are coming up with are simply outrageous, but there is no one challenging them, questioning them, or fighting them. Most major industries have groups that can represent the best interests for their members. For example, when President Trump was still a candidate, he kept talking about tax reform—making the tax laws simpler so that anybody could understand them and people could just file their tax returns on a postcard. That may be nice for individual taxpayers, but for me as a CPA, that would be detrimental to my business. So the lobbyists for the CPA industry, the American Institute for Certified Public Accountants (AICPA), went to Washington and advocated against such an extreme change to the nation's tax laws. I had a lobbying group looking out for my best interests as a CPA and businessman, and merchants like you need this too.

In order to protect your interests, merchants like yourself need to organize and lobby the federal and state governments to stop passing laws and regulations that are detrimental to the e-commerce industry. Having an organized lobbying group to represent you can go a long way; these are groups that lawmakers genuinely listen to. Online Merchants Guild is a group that has begun to receive some significant media attention, and it would be worth it for you to consider joining the group. You can find more information about the guild at

https://onlinemerchantsguild.org/.

24
A Possible Option for Sales Tax Reform

One solution that would reduce the cost of compliance to online sellers while still allowing states to collect the sales tax money due to them is to have the marketplace facilitators—e.g., Amazon—collect and remit the sales tax. This is similar to what Amazon is doing in Washington, except ideally third-party sellers without any additional sales tax obligations to the state would not even have to file sales tax returns—Amazon would simply file the return. States like Washington got greedy. What is absurd about Washington's tax laws is that a seller still has to file a return, even if the seller's only sales are through Amazon; the portion of sales tax that Amazon paid is taken as a deduction. The money never touches the hands of the seller. It goes from the buyer, through Amazon, to the state. Yet the state of Washington requires merchants to file a tax return indicating how much Amazon paid on their behalf.

Having Amazon collect and remit sales tax on behalf of all of its third-party merchants makes sense; after all, Amazon already collects and remits sales tax for all of its own sales. Unlike small third-party merchants, Amazon already has the internal infrastructure set up to handle complex sales tax returns. Amazon already collects and remits sales taxes in every state that levies a sales tax, so the relative increase in the burden would be minimal, as compared to the significant burden placed on small businesses. With this solution, the cost of compliance would go right out the window for online merchants. Without having to worry about determining nexus, registering for tax permits, and filing tax returns, small business owners could focus on actually running their businesses.

Washington can get away with its current law because no one is advocating on behalf of online sellers and merchants. If other states see that a law like Washington's actually works and brings in more venue, it is only going to get increasingly difficult for online merchants to survive. Merchants will be forced into registering in nearly every state, even if their tax burden in those states is minimal, and businesses are going to be overcome by the astronomical costs of compliance. This is why it is so important that small business owners operating online band together to challenge proposed legislation and regulations that would be harmful to the e-commerce industry.

25
Common Bookkeeping Mistakes

A common problem among small business owners, especially e-commerce sellers, is that they start selling and see the money begin to come flowing in, but they do not have a bookkeeping system in place—or maybe they have a bookkeeping system, but it is not set up properly. This is especially important for third-party sellers on Amazon, because once you start your business on Amazon, your sales can go through the roof. You can really quickly go from being a small business to a medium-sized business (or even a large business, if you are fortunate).

At the point that you become a medium-sized business with a fair amount of sales, you need to start actually treating it like a business. It does not matter if you are still operating out of your garage or if you are actually set up in a warehouse or have a small office; you need to start thinking like other business people. This means that you need to have accounting and bookkeeping systems in place; a lot of the decision that you will have to make are going to be based off of numbers, and if those numbers are incorrect, the decisions that you are making for your business are not going to be as accurate as you need them to be. That can be very harmful to your business.

As an example, one of the biggest mistakes people make while doing their own bookkeeping is that at the point they buy inventory or make purchases to sell on Amazon, they immediately treat it as an expense. This is incorrect; inventory cannot be expensed until it is actually sold. This means that as you spend money to purchase inventory, you are not getting a deduction. It should be going into an asset account called "inventory." Only at the point that you sell that inventory can you expense it.

A second mistake that Amazon merchants commonly make is basing their sales numbers off of the amount of money they receive from Amazon. They get a direct deposit from Amazon every two weeks, and at the end of the year they add up all those Amazon payments and use that number as their annual sales. The error here is that Amazon pays merchants after having already taken out their fees. A merchant's total annual sales number is always going to be higher than the amount the merchant actually received from Amazon. Amazon knows what that actual number is, and that is the number that they report to the IRS on a 1099-K. The amount reported on Form 1099-K tells a merchant—and the IRS—how much the merchant's sales were before Amazon took out their fees. When you file your tax return, if you just add up the totals from looking at direct deposits from Amazon in your checking account, that number will not match the number that Amazon listed on the 1099-K, and that is going to raise a major red flag with the IRS. You need to ensure that you are going through Amazon Seller Central and looking at the revenue number before Amazon takes its fees out; this will ensure that you are keeping accurate records for tax purposes.

If you decide to handle your bookkeeping on your own, you will almost certainly want to utilize some sort of bookkeeping software. There are a variety of software options out there, and it is worth your time to research what software package will best fit your needs. As discussed in Chapter 4, TaxJar and Avalara are two popular companies providing software/application solutions specifically for sales tax purposes.

26
Avoiding an Audit from the IRS

There is a lot of information out there available—especially on the internet—for small business owners to look at; while this free information may be helpful at a general level, the best way to get advice tailored to meet the specific needs of you and your business is to talk to a certified public accountant. There are a lot of people out there who are accountants, and there are people out there who are just bookkeepers. These people may know the relevant rules and regulations, and they can probably perform a general overview of your business's numbers, but the best option to ensure that you are talking to someone who knows the rules and regulations in and out is to consult with a CPA who is familiar with online retailers. A CPA is generally going to be better than a non-licensed accountant, since CPAs have to pass an exam, be licensed with the state, and participate in continuing professional education to keep their license.

That being said, there are CPAs out there who are not well suited to handle questions related to online retailers like Amazon merchants. Think about the field of CPAs like the medical field. If you had a broken arm, your initial thought would be that you need to go to a doctor. But the type of doctor you go to matters. If you went to a dermatologist and said, "Fix this; you're a doctor," the dermatologist would look at you and say, "I don't know how to fix that; I only work with skin. Go to a different doctor." The same thing applies to CPAs. There are CPAs out there who know how to work with Amazon and e-commerce sellers, but there are plenty of CPAs out there who lack a sufficient understanding in how e-commerce systems work or the laws unique to the e-commerce industry. As states are passing more "Amazon laws" and finding new ways to target online merchants, the statutes and regulations related to the industry are getting more complex and increasing in number. This is why it is crucial that you make sure you are getting advice from a professional who knows what he or she is talking about.

Do more than just what most other e-commerce merchants are doing. Going on Facebook and asking a question hoping to get the right answer from someone who claims to know is not a smart solution. While there may be websites out there that provide helpful information, an article or blog post is going to be broad in subject and may not address specific issues relevant to your situation. You need to make sure that you can trust that the professional advising you knows what he or she is talking about and is accurately advising you on all of your accounting and tax situations.

A Note from the Author

I hope this book has been beneficial in enhancing your understanding of how sales tax laws impact your business. Getting everything started and set up the correct way is very important, and it is never too late to change things to ensure that you are doing them correctly—regardless of how long you have been selling on Amazon.

I am a CPA and the owner of EDIZ Accounting. I have years of experience helping Amazon sellers—from merchants with large accounts and high volumes of sales to newer Amazon sellers who are just starting out or have not yet even formed their business. You can check out my website at ebizaccounting.com or reach me at my office at (914) 664-1900. If you are looking for a CPA or just have general questions about sales tax or the topics covered in this book, I would encourage you to give me a call or visit my website.

Again, thank you for taking the time to read through this book; I truly hope it was helpful, and I wish you the best of luck in your business ventures.

—Tim Nelson, CPA

Appendix

Sales Tax Rates and Contact Information for State Sales Tax Authorities

(This information is subject to change; always check with the appropriate government entity or a tax professional to ensure that you are complying with all current laws)

Alaska

No state sales tax but allows for local sales taxes

Alabama

Sales Tax Rate: 4% (also allows for local sales taxes)

Agency: Alabama Department of Revenue

Address: 50 North Ripley Street, Montgomery, AL 36104

Website: https://revenue.alabama.gov/sales-use/taxes-administered/sales-tax/

Phone: (334) 242-1490

Register Online: My Alabama Taxes (MAT) – https://myalabamataxes.alabama.gov/_/

Arizona

Sales Tax Rate: 5.6% (also allows for local sales taxes)

Agency: Arizona Department of Revenue

Address: 1600 West Monroe Street, Phoenix, AZ 85007

Website: https://azdor.gov/

Phone: (602) 255-3381

Register Online: https://www.aztaxes.gov/Security/Register

Arkansas

Sales Tax Rate: 6.5% (also allows for local sales taxes)

Agency: Arkansas Department of Finance and Administration

Address: 1509 West 7th Street, Little Rock, AR 72201

Website: https://www.dfa.arkansas.gov/

Phone: (501) 682-7104

Email: Sales.tax@dfa.arkansas.gov

Register Online: Arkansas Taxpayer Access Point (ATAP) – https://atap.arkansas.gov/_/#7

California

Sales Tax Rate: 7.25% (also allows for local sales taxes)

Agency: California Department of Tax and Fee Administration

Address: 450 N Street, Sacramento, CA 95814

Website: http://www.cdtfa.ca.gov/

Phone: (800) 400-7115

Register Online: http://www.cdtfa.ca.gov/services/

Colorado

Sales Tax Rate: 2.9% (also allows for local sales taxes)

Agency: Colorado Department of Revenue

Address: 1375 Sherman Street, Denver, CO 80261

Website: https://www.colorado.gov/tax

Phone: (303) 238-7378

Register Online: MyBizColorado – https://mybiz.colorado.gov/intro (only for in-state businesses with a single location)

Connecticut

Sales Tax Rate: 6.35%

Agency: Connecticut Department of Revenue

Address: 450 Columbus Boulevard, Suite 1, Hartford, CT 06103

Website: https://www.ct.gov/drs/site/default.asp

Phone: (860) 297-5962

Email: drs@po.state.ct.us

Register Online: Connecticut Taxpayer Services Center – https://www.ct.gov/drs/cwp/view.asp?a=1433&q=265880

Delaware

No state or local sales taxes; however, the state does impose a gross receipts tax

Florida

Sales Tax Rate: 6% (also allows for local sales taxes)

Agency: Florida Department of Revenue

Address: 5050 West Tennessee Street, Tallahassee, FL 32399

Website: http://floridarevenue.com/taxes/tax-esfees/Pages/sales_tax.aspx

Phone: (850) 488-6800

Email: DORGTA@floridarevenue.com

Register Online: http://floridarevenue.com/taxes/eserv-ices/Pages/registration.aspx

Georgia

Sales Tax Rate: 4% (also allows for local sales taxes)

Agency: Georgia Department of Revenue

Address: 1800 Century Boulevard NE, Atlanta, GA 30345

Website: https://dor.georgia.gov/sales-use-tax

Phone: (877) 423-6711

Register Online: Georgia Tax Center –
https://gtc.dor.ga.gov/_/#2

Hawaii

General Excise Tax Rate: 6% (also allows for local sales taxes)

Agency: Hawaii Department of Taxation

Address: 830 Punchbowl Street, Honolulu, HI 96813

Website: http://tax.hawaii.gov/

Phone: (808) 587-4242

Email: Taxpayer.Services@hawaii.gov

Register Online: Hawaii Business Express – https://hbe.eha-waii.gov/BizEx/home.eb

Idaho

Sales Tax Rate: 6% (also allows for local sales taxes)

Agency: Idaho State Tax Commission

Mailing Address: PO Box 36, Boise, ID 83722-0410

Website: https://tax.idaho.gov/i-1049.cfm

Phone: (800) 972-7660

Register Online: Idaho Business Registration System (IBR) – https://labor.idaho.gov/ibrs/ibr.aspx

Illinois

Sales Tax Rate: 6.25% (also allows for local sales taxes)

Agency: Illinois Revenue

Address: James R. Thompson Center – Concourse Level, 100 West Randolph Street,
Chicago, IL 60601

Website: http://tax.illinois.gov/businesses/taxinfor-mation/sales/rot.htm

Phone: (800) 732-8866

Register Online: MyTaxIllinois – https://mytax.illinois.gov/_/

Indiana

Sales Tax Rate: 7%

Agency: Indiana Department of Revenue

Website: https://www.in.gov/dor/3986.htm

Phone: (317) 233-4015

Email: businesstaxassistance@dor.in.gov

Register Online: INTax – https://www.in.gov/dor/4336.htm

Iowa

Sales Tax Rate: 6% (also allows for local sales taxes)

Agency: Iowa Department of Revenue

Address: Hoover State Office Building – 4th Floor, 1305 East Walnut, Des Moines, IA 50319

Website: https://tax.iowa.gov/

Phone: (800) 367-3388

Register Online: https://www.idr.iowa.gov/CBA/start.asp

Kansas

Sales Tax Rate: 6.5% (also allows for local sales taxes)

Agency: Kansas Department of Revenue

Address: Scott State Office Building, 120 SE 10th Street, Topeka, KS 66612

Website: https://www.ksrevenue.org/index.html

Phone: (785) 368-8222

Email: kdor_tac@ks.gov

Register Online: https://www.kdor.ks.gov/apps/kcsc/login.aspx

Kentucky

Sales Tax Rate: 6%

Agency: Kentucky Department of Revenue

Address: 501 High Street, Frankfort, KY 40601

Website: https://revenue.ky.gov/Pages/index.aspx

Phone: (502) 564-5170

Register Online: Kentucky Business One Stop Portal – https://onestop.ky.gov/Pages/default.aspx

Louisiana

Sales Tax Rate: 5% (also allows for local sales taxes)

Agency: Louisiana Department of Revenue

Address: 617 North Third Street, Baton Rouge, LA 70802

Website: http://www.revenue.louisiana.gov/Businesses

Phone: (855) 307-3893

Register Online: geauxBiz – https://geauxbiz.sos.la.gov/

Maine

Sales Tax Rate: 5.5%

Agency: Maine Revenue Services

Address: 51 Commerce Drive, Augusta, ME 04330

Website: https://www.maine.gov/revenue/salesuse/sales-tax/salestax.html

Phone: (207) 624-9693

Email: sales.tax@maine.gov

Register Online: Sales & Use, Withholding and Service Provider Tax Registration Service – https://www5.informe.org/cgi-bin/online/suwtaxreg/index

Maryland

Sales Tax Rate: 6%

Agency: Comptroller of Maryland

Address: 60 West Street, Suite 102, Annapolis, MD 21401

Website: https://taxes.marylandtaxes.gov/Business_Taxes/Busi-
ness_Tax_Types/
Sales_and_Use_Tax/default.shtml

Phone: (800) 638-2937

Email: sut@comp.state.md.us

Register Online: https://interactive.mary-
landtaxes.gov/webapps/comptrollercra/entrance.asp

Massachusetts

Sales Tax Rate: 6.25%

Agency: Massachusetts Department of Revenue

Address: 100 Cambridge Street, Boston, MA 02114

Website: https://www.mass.gov/guides/sales-and-use-tax

Phone: (617) 887-6367

Register Online: MassTax Connect –
https://mtc.dor.state.ma.us/mtc/_/#2

Michigan

Sales Tax Rate: 6%

Agency: Michigan Department of Treasury

Mailing Address: Michigan Department of Treasury, Lansing, MI 48922

Website: https://www.michigan.gov/taxes/0,4676,7-238-43519_43529---,00.html

Phone: (517) 373-3200

Register Online: https://www.michigan.gov/uia/0,1607,7-118--89978--,00.html

Minnesota

Sales Tax Rate: 6.875% (also allows for local sales taxes)

Agency: Minnesota Department of Revenue

Address: 600 North Robert Street, St. Paul, MN 55146

Website: http://www.revenue.state.mn.us/businesses/sut/Pages/File-and-Pay.aspx

Phone: (651) 296-6181

Email: salesuse.tax@state.mn.us

Register Online: MN eServices –
https://www.mndor.state.mn.us/tp/eservices/_/

Mississippi

Sales Tax Rate: 7% (also allows for local sales taxes)

Agency: Mississippi Department of Revenue

Address: 500 Clinton Center Drive, Clinton, MS 39056

Website: http://www.dor.ms.gov/Business/Pages/Sales-Use-Tax-landing.aspx

Phone: (601) 923-7015

Register Online: Taxpayer Access Point (TAP) – https://tap.dor.ms.gov/_/

Missouri

Sales Tax Rate: 4.225% (also allows for local sales taxes)

Agency: Missouri Department of Revenue

Address: Harry S Truman State Office Building, 301 West High Street, Jefferson City, MO 65101

Website: https://dor.mo.gov/business/sales/

Phone: (573) 751-4450

Email: salesuse@dor.mo.gov

Register Online: MyTax Missouri – https://dor.mo.gov/register-business/index.php

Montana

No state or local sales taxes

Nebraska

Sales Tax Rate: 5.5% (also allows for local sales taxes)

Agency: Nebraska Department of Revenue

Address: Nebraska State Office Building, 301 Centennial Mall S, Lincoln, NE 68508

Website: http://www.revenue.nebraska.gov/salestax.html

Phone: (402) 471-5729

Register Online: http://www.revenue.nebraska.gov/electron/online_f20.html

Nevada

Sales Tax Rate: 6.85% (also allows for local sales taxes)

Agency: Nevada Department of Taxation

Address: 1550 College Parkway, Suite 115, Carson City, NV 89706

Website: https://tax.nv.gov/

Phone: (866) 962-3707

Register Online: Nevada Tax Center – https://www.nevada-tax.nv.gov/

New Hampshire

No state or local sales taxes

New Jersey

Sales Tax Rate: 6.625%

Agency: New Jersey Department of the Treasury

Address: 50 Barrack Street, Trenton, NJ 08695

Website: https://www.state.nj.us/treasury/taxation/su.shtml

Phone: (609) 292-6400

Register Online: https://www.njportal.com/DOR/BusinessRegistration/

New Mexico

Sales Tax Rate: 5.125% (also allows for local sales taxes)

Agency: New Mexico Taxation & Revenue Department

Address: 1100 South St. Francis Drive, Santa Fe, NM 87504

Website: http://www.tax.newmexico.gov/Default.aspx

Phone: (505) 827-0832

Register Online: Taxpayer Access Point (TAP) – https://tap.state.nm.us/tap/_/

New York

Sales Tax Rate: 4% (also allows for local sales taxes)

Agency: New York Department of Taxation and Finance

Address: Harriman Campus Road, Albany, NY 12226

Website: https://www.tax.ny.gov/bus/st/stidx.htm

Phone: (518) 485-2889

Register Online: https://www.ny.gov/services/licenses

Oregon

No state or local sales taxes

North Carolina

Sales Tax Rate: 4.75% (also allows for local sales taxes)

Agency: North Carolina Department of Revenue

Address: 501 North Wilmington Street, Raleigh, NC 27604

Website: https://www.ncdor.gov/

Phone: (877) 252-3052

Register Online: https://www.ncdor.gov/taxes-forms/business-registration/online-business-registration

North Dakota

Sales Tax Rate: 5% (also allows for local sales taxes)

Agency: North Dakota Office of State Tax Commissioner

Address: 600 E. Boulevard Avenue, Bismarck, ND 58505-0599

Website: https://www.nd.gov/tax/

Phone: (701) 328-1246

Email: salestax@nd.gov

Register Online: Taxpayer Access Point (TAP) –
https://apps.nd.gov/tax/tap/_/

Ohio

Sales Tax Rate: 5.75% (also allows for local sales taxes)

Agency: Ohio Department of Taxation

Address: 4485 Northland Ridge Boulevard, Columbus, OH 43229

Website: https://www.tax.ohio.gov/sales_and_use.aspx

Phone: (888) 405-4039

Register Online: Ohio Business Gateway –
https://www.tax.ohio.gov/online_services/ohio_business_gate-
way_2_0.aspx

Pennsylvania

Sales Tax Rate: 6% (also allows for local sales taxes)

Agency: Pennsylvania Department of Revenue

Mailing Address: Bureau of Business Trust Fund Taxes, PO Box 280905, Harrisburg, PA 17128-0905

Website: https://www.revenue.pa.gov/Pages/default.aspx

Phone: (717) 787-1064

Register Online: Online PA100 – https://www.pa100.state.pa.us/Registration.htm

Rhode Island

Sales Tax Rate: 7%

Agency: Rhode Island Division of Taxation

Address: One Capitol Hill, Providence, RI 02908

Website: http://www.tax.ri.gov/regulations/salestax/

Phone: (401) 574-8955

Email: Tax.Excise@tax.ri.gov

Register Online: https://www.ri.gov/taxation/BAR/

South Carolina

Sales Tax Rate: 6% (also allows for local sales taxes)

Agency: South Carolina Department of Revenue

Address: 300A Outlet Pointe Boulevard, Columbia, SC 29210

Website: https://dor.sc.gov/tax/sales-and-use

Phone: (803) 898-5000

Email: SalesTax@dor.sc.gov

Register Online: MyDORWAY – https://dor.sc.gov/mydorway

South Dakota

Sales Tax Rate: 4.5% (also allows for local sales taxes)

Agency: South Dakota Department of Revenue

Address: 445 E Capitol Avenue, Pierre, SD 57501

Website: http://dor.sd.gov/

Phone: (800) 829-9188

Email: bustax@state.sd.us

Register Online: https://apps.sd.gov/rv23cedar/main/main.aspx

Tennessee

Sales Tax Rate: 7% (also allows for local sales taxes)

Agency: Tennessee Department of Revenue

Address: 500 Deaderick Street, Nashville, TN 37242

Website: https://www.tn.gov/revenue/taxes/sales-and-use-tax.html

Phone: (615) 253-0600

Register Online: Tennessee Taxpayer Access Point (TNTAP) – https://tntap.tn.gov/EServices/_/

Texas

Sales Tax Rate: 6.25% (also allows for local sales taxes)

Agency: Texas Comptroller of Public Accounts

Address: Lyndon B. Johnson State Office Building, 111 East 17th Street, Austin, TX 78774

Website: https://comptroller.texas.gov/taxes/sales/

Phone: (800) 252-5555

Register Online: https://comptroller.texas.gov/taxes/permit/

Utah

Sales Tax Rate: 4.7% (also allows for local sales taxes)

Agency: Utah State Tax Commission

Address: 210 North 1950 West, Salt Lake City, UT 84134

Website: https://tax.utah.gov/sales

Phone: (800) 662-4335

Email: taxmaster@utah.gov

Register Online: OneStop Business Registration System - https://secure.utah.gov/account/log-in.html

Vermont

Sales Tax Rate: 6% (also allows for local sales taxes)

Agency: Vermont Department of Taxes

Address: 133 State Street, Montpelier, VT 05633

Website: http://tax.vermont.gov/

Phone: (802) 828-2551

Email: tax.business@vermont.gov

Register Online: http://tax.vermont.gov/business-and-corp/register-renew-close-business

Virginia

Sales Tax Rate: 4.3% (also allows for local sales taxes)

Agency: Virginia Department of Taxation

Mailing Address: Virginia Tax, Office of Customer Services, PO Box 1115, Richmond, VA 23218-1115

Website: https://tax.virginia.gov/

Phone: (804) 367-8037

Register Online: https://www.ireg.tax.virginia.gov/VTOL/Login.seam

Washington

Sales Tax Rate: 6.5% (also allows for local sales taxes)

Agency: Washington Department of Revenue

Website: https://dor.wa.gov/find-taxes-rates/sales-and-use-tax-rates

Phone: (800) 647-7706

Register Online: http://bls.dor.wa.gov/

Washington, DC

Sales Tax Rate: 5.75%

Agency: Office of Tax and Revenue

Mailing Address: 1101 4th Street, SW, Suite 270 West, Washington, DC 20024

Website: https://otr.cfo.dc.gov/

Phone: (202) 727-4829

Register Online: MyTax DC – https://mytax.dc.gov/_/

West Virginia

Sales Tax Rate: 6% (also allows for local sales taxes)

Agency: West Virginia State Tax Department

Address: The Revenue Center, 1001 Lee Street East, Charleston, WV 25301

Website: https://tax.wv.gov/Pages/default.aspx

Phone: (800) 982-8297

Email: TaxHelp@WV.Gov

Register Online: https://www.business4wv.com/b4wvpublic/default.aspx

Wisconsin

Sales Tax Rate: 5% (also allows for local sales taxes)

Agency: Wisconsin Department of Revenue

Address: 2135 Rimrock Road, Madison, WI 53713

Website: https://www.reve-nue.wi.gov/Pages/SalesAndUse/Home.aspx

Phone: (608) 266-2776

Register Online: https://www.revenue.wi.gov/Pages/Busi-nesses/New-Business-home.aspx

Wyoming

Sales Tax Rate: 4% (also allows for local sales taxes)

Agency: Wyoming Department of Revenue

Address: 122 West 25th Street, 2nd Floor West, Cheyenne, WY 82002

Website: http://revenue.wyo.gov/Excise-Tax-Division

Phone: (307) 777-5200

Email: dor@wyo.gov

Register Online: https://excise-wyifs.wy.gov/

Economic Nexus Thresholds by State

(This information is subject to change; always check with the appropriate government entity or a tax professional to ensure that you are complying with all current laws)

Alabama

$250,000 in sales per year, based on the previous calendar year

Arkansas

Legislation Pending

Colorado

$100,000 per year in gross revenue OR 200 separate transactions, based on the previous or current calendar year

Connecticut

(Effective date: December 1, 2018)

$250,000 per year in gross revenue AND 200 separate transactions, based on the previous calendar year

Georgia

(Effective date: January 1, 2019)

$250,000 per year in gross revenue AND 200 separate transactions, based on the previous or current calendar year

Hawaii

$100,000 per year in gross revenue OR 200 separate transactions, based on the previous or current calendar year

Illinois

$100,000 per year in gross revenue OR 200 separate transactions, based on the previous twelve months

Indiana

$100,000 per year in gross revenue OR 200 separate transactions, based on the previous calendar year

Iowa

(Effective date: January 1, 2019)

$100,000 per year in gross revenue OR 200 separate transactions, based on the previous or current calendar year

Kentucky

$100,000 per year in gross revenue OR 200 separate transactions, based on the previous or current calendar year

Louisiana

(Effective date: January 1, 2019)

$100,000 per year in gross revenue OR 200 separate transactions, based on the previous or current calendar year

Maine

$100,000 per year in gross revenue OR 200 separate transactions, based on the previous or current calendar year

Maryland

$100,000 per year in gross revenue OR 200 separate transactions, based on the previous or current calendar year

Massachusetts

$500,000 per year in gross revenue AND 100 separate transactions, based on the previous calendar year

Michigan

$100,000 per year in gross revenue OR 200 separate transactions, based on the previous calendar year

Minnesota

$100,000 per year in gross revenue, based on the previous or current calendar year OR 100 separate transactions, based on the previous twelve months

Mississippi

$250,000 sales, based on the previous twelve months

Nebraska

(Effective date: January 1, 2019)

$100,000 per year in sales OR 200 separate transactions per year

New Jersey

$100,000 per year in gross revenue OR 200 separate transactions, based on the previous or current calendar year

North Carolina

(Effective date: November 1, 2018)

$100,000 per year in gross revenue OR 200 separate transactions, based on the previous or current calendar year

North Dakota

$100,000 per year in gross revenue OR 200 separate transactions, based on the previous or current calendar year

Oklahoma

$10,000 per year in sales, based on the previous 12 months; must either collect sales tax or comply with the state's notice and report law

Pennsylvania

$10,000 per year in sales, based on the previous 12 months; must either collect sales tax or comply with the state's notice and report law

Rhode Island

$10,000 per year in sales or 200 separate transactions, based on a calendar year; must either collect sales tax or comply with the state's notice and report law

South Carolina

(Effective date: November 1, 2018)

$100,000 per year in sales, based on the previous or current calendar year

South Dakota

(Effective date: November 1, 2018)

$100,000 per year in sales OR 200 separate transactions, based on the previous or current calendar year

Tennessee

$500,000 in sales in the previous twelve months

Utah

(Effective date: January 1, 2019)

$100,000 per year in sales OR 200 separate transactions, based on the previous or current calendar year

Vermont

$100,000 per year in sales OR 200 separate transactions during any preceding twelve-month period

Washington

$10,000 per year in sales; must either collect sales tax or comply with the state's notice and report law

Wisconsin

$100,000 per year in sales OR 200 separate transactions per year

Wyoming

$100,000 per year in sales OR 200 separate transactions, based on the previous or current calendar year

Click-Through Nexus Thresholds by State

(This information is subject to change; always check with the appropriate government entity or a tax professional to ensure that you are complying with all current laws)

Alabama

$10,000 based on the previous twelve months

Rebuttable presumption

California

$10,000 based on the previous twelve months; total annual in-state sales must also exceed $1,000,000

Rebuttable presumption

Connecticut

$2,000 based on the previous four quarters

Irrebuttable presumption

Georgia

$50,000 based on the previous twelve months

Rebuttable presumption

Idaho

$10,000 based on the previous twelve months

Rebuttable presumption

Kansas

$10,000 based on the previous twelve months

Rebuttable presumption

Louisiana

$50,000 based on the previous twelve months

Rebuttable presumption

Maine

$10,000 based on the previous twelve months

Rebuttable presumption

Michigan

$10,000 based on the previous twelve months

Rebuttable presumption

Minnesota

$10,000 based on the twelve-month period ending on the last day of the most recent quarter

Rebuttable presumption

Missouri

$10,000 based on the previous twelve months

Rebuttable presumption

Nevada

$10,000 based on the previous four quarters

Rebuttable presumption

New Jersey

$10,000 based on the previous four quarters

Rebuttable presumption

New York

$10,000 based on the previous four quarters

Rebuttable presumption

North Carolina

$10,000 based on the previous four quarters

Rebuttable presumption

Ohio

$10,000 based on the previous calendar year

Rebuttable presumption

Pennsylvania

Any amount

Rhode Island

$10,000 based on the previous four quarters

Rebuttable presumption

Tennessee

$10,000 based on the previous twelve months

Rebuttable presumption

Vermont

$10,000 based on the previous tax year

Rebuttable presumption

Washington

$10,000 based on the previous tax year

Rebuttable presumption

Glossary

Accountant – a financial professional who reviews finances of individuals and/or businesses

Affiliate nexus – nexus established with a state by an out-of-state merchant using an in-state individual or business for services related to the merchant's sales

Amazon laws – sales tax laws targeted to capture tax revenue from online retailers; laws related to click-through nexus, affiliate nexus, and notice and report requirements are all examples of Amazon laws

Amazon Fulfillment Center – warehouses owned and run by Amazon where merchants' inventory is stored and shipped from; having inventory in a fulfillment center creates nexus with the state in which the center is located

Amazon Sort center – locations run by Amazon to which a package is sent to be sorted to speed up delivery time; at the point the package reaches the sort center, the buyer is the owner of the contents, so a sort center by itself does not create nexus for the merchant

Audit – an examination and evaluation of the financial records and statements of an individual or organization

Auditor – an individual who reviews and verifies the accuracy of financial records

Click-through nexus – nexus established with a by an out-of-state merchant contracting with individuals or companies in the state to refer customers to the merchant through a web link for a commission or other compensation

Corporation – a legal entity that is authorized to act as a single entity and is distinct and separate from its owners

Certified public accountant (CPA) – an accountant who has passed a state licensing exam and is licensed with the state

Economic nexus – nexus established by a business conducting economic activity in a state, usually established by exceeding a threshold of sales in dollar amount and/or transaction number

Fulfillment by Amazon (FBA) – a service for Amazon sellers where the seller ships inventory to Amazon and Amazon packages and ships the products to buyers on behalf of the seller

Franchise tax – a tax levied by a state on businesses with nexus with the state; the amount owed is usually a flat annual fee based on annual income

Gross receipts tax (or gross excise tax) – a tax levied on the gross revenue of a company; as opposed to a sales tax, it is levied on the seller

Income tax – a tax levied on the income of an individual or business

Limited liability partnership (LLP) – a partnership in which some or all partners have limited liability

Limited partnership (LP) – a partnership that consists of at least one general partner and one limited partner; the limited partner(s) have limited liability

Limited liability company (LLC) – a hybrid business entity combining elements of a corporation and partnership (or sole proprietorship if there is only a single owner); it is similar to a corporation with respect to limited liability but similar to a partnership (or sole proprietorship) for income tax purposes

Look-back period – the period of time for which a business or individual can be held liable for unpaid tax liabilities

Marketplace facilitator law – a law requiring online marketplaces to collect and remit sales tax on behalf of merchants selling on the marketplace's platform

Nexus – connections with a state that render an out-of-state merchant liable for sales tax purposes; while traditionally this was established by having a sufficient physical presence in a state, states may establish nexus through other legislatively defined means

Notice and report law – a law requiring online retailers to notify buyers of a state's use tax requirements; under some laws, a retailer may be required to send buyers an annual statement of all purchases from the retailer

Partnership – an association of two or more people to carry on a business for profit; all partners are jointly and severally liable and jointly own the business

Pass-through tax – a tax related to business activity that is not paid by the business

S corporation – a closely held corporation that has chosen to be taxed under Subchapter S of Chapter 1 of the Internal Revenue Code; instead of S corporations paying income taxes, any tax obligations (or losses) are passed through to the S corporation's shareholders

Sales tax – a consumption tax levied on the sale of goods and/or services

Sole proprietorship – a business owned and run by a single person; there is no distinction between the owner and the business entity

Tax attorney – an individual who has passed a state bar exam and is licensed to practice law in the state who specializes in tax law

Use tax – a tax levied on items purchased out of state that will be used, stored, or consumed in the state where the consumer resides and on which no tax was collected when purchased

Voluntary Disclosure Agreement (VDA) – a binding agreement between a taxpayer and the state, wherein the taxpayer receives benefits, such as reduced or waived penalties or a limited look-back period, in exchange for the taxpayer proactively disclosing prior unpaid tax liabilities

References

Affiliate Nexus and the Out-of-State Seller, AVALARA, https://www.avalara.com/us/en/learn/whitepapers/affiliate-nexus-state-seller.html (last visited Sept. 28, 2018).

Amazon Laws and Click-Through Nexus, VERTEX, https://www.vertexinc.com/resources/insights/amazon-laws-and-click-through-nexus (last visited Sept. 27, 2018).

Direct Mktg Ass'n v. Brohl, 135 S. Ct. 1124 (2015).

FBA Inventory Placement Service, AMAZON, https://sellercentral.amazon.com/gp/help/external/200735910?language=en-US&ref=mpbc_201233560_cont_200735910 (last visited Sept. 30, 2018).

Income Tax Nexus 101 – Can That State Really Impose a Tax on My Company's Income? Really?, BINGHAM GREENEBAUM DOLL LLP (Aug. 1, 2011), https://www.bgdlegal.com/blog/income-tax-nexus-101-can-that-state.

Interstate Income Act of 1959, 15 U.S.C. §§ 381–384 (2018).

Introduction & Tax Strategy (FAQ), ONLINE MERCHANTS GUILD, https://onlinemerchantsguild.org/faq/ (last visited Sept. 30, 2018).

Is My Corporation Subject to Franchise Tax or Income Tax?, ST. CAL. FRANCHISE TAX BOARD (Dec. 18, 2017), https://www.ftb.ca.gov/businesses/faq/734.shtml.

Nat'l Bellas Hess, Inc. v. Dep't of Revenue of Illinois, 386 U.S. 753 (1967).

Nw. States Portland Cement Co. v. Minnesota, 358 U.S. 450 (1959).

Online Merchants Guild... The Future of Ecommerce Merchant Sales?, MEDIA HORIZONS (May 3, 2018), https://www.mediahorizons.com/online-merchants-guild-the-future-of-ecommerce-merchant-sales/.

Personal Liability for Sales Tax - Not Just for Corporate Officers Anymore!, ACCOUNTINGWEB (Oct. 9, 2017), https://www.accountingweb.com/tax/sales-tax/personal-liability-for-sales-tax-not-just-for-corporate-officers-anymore.

Quill Corp. v. North Dakota, 504 U.S. 298 (1992).

Remote Seller Nexus Chart, SALES TAX INST. (Sept. 20, 2018), https://www.salestaxinstitute.com/resources/remote-seller-nexus-chart.

S.B. 106, 2016 Leg., 91st Sess. (S.D. 2016).

South Dakota v. Wayfair, Inc., 138 S. Ct. 2080 (2018).

Use Stores to Showcase Your Brand, AMAZON ADVERTISING (July 25, 2017), https://advertising.amazon.com/blog/amazon-stores.

When to Register for a Sales Tax License, TAXJAR (June 14, 2016), https://www.taxjar.com/guides/register-for-sales-tax/#introduction.

Kerry Alexander, *The Tax You Probably Owe, but Aren't Paying: A Closer Look at Consumer Use Tax Compliance*, AVALARA (Jan. 28, 2016), https://www.avalara.com/us/en/blog/2016/01/the-tax-you-probably-owe-but-arent-paying-a-closer-look-at-consumer-use-tax-compliance.html.

Michael Bannasch, *Factor Presence Nexus: A Growing Trend in State Taxation*, J. ACCT. (July 1, 2017), https://www.journalofaccountancy.com/issues/2017/jul/state-taxation-presence-nexus.html.

Mark Berens, *From Concrete to the Cloud: 5 Events That Shaped US Nexus Law*, AVALARA: TRUSTFILE (Mar. 18, 2106), https://www.avalara.com/trustfile/en/blog/from-concrete-to-the-cloud-5-events-that-shaped-us-nexus-law.html.

Matthew C. Boch, Way*(un)*fair? *United States Supreme Court Decision Ends State Tax Physical Presence Nexus Test*, ARK. LAW., Summer 2018, at 18.

Marc Brandeis & Daniel W. Layton, South Dakota v. Wayfair*: From* International Shoe *to Interstate Sales Tax*, 60 ORANGE COUNTY LAW., September 2018, at 32.

Amanda Cameron, *What Small Business Owners Need to Know About Pass-through Taxation*, PATRIOT SOFTWARE: ACCOUNTING BLOG (Mar. 30, 2017), https://www.patriotsoftware.com/accounting/training/blog/what-is-pass-through-taxation-entity-benefits/.

Gail Cole, *Amazon and Etsy Are Complying with Washington's Marketplace Sales Tax Law: What That Means for Sellers*, AVALARA (Jan. 15, 2018), https://www.avalara.com/us/en/blog/2018/01/amazon-etsy-complying-washingtons-marketplace-sales-tax-law-means-sellers.html.

Gail Cole, *Debunking 4 Myths About Voluntary Disclosure Agreements*, AVALARA (May 18, 2018), https://www.avalara.com/us/en/blog/2018/05/debunking-4-mythsaboutvoluntarydisclosureagreements.html.

Sylvia F. Dion, *Tax Treaties and U.S. Sales Tax Nexus: What Foreign Sellers Need to Know*, SALESTAXSUPPORT.COM (June 18, 2013), https://www.salestaxsupport.com/blogs/industry/us-sales-tax-for-foreign-sellers/tax-treaties-us-sales-tax-nexus-foreign-sellers/.

Sylvia F. Dion, *Wayfair & Economic Nexus for Foreign Sellers: Key Sales Tax Questions*, SALESTAXSUPPORT.COM (Aug. 10, 2018), https://www.salestaxsupport.com/blogs/industry/us-sales-tax-for-foreign-sellers/wayfair-economic-nexus-for-foreign-sellers-sales-tax-questions/.

Jennifer Dunn, *Amazon and Etsy (But Not Walmart) Will Now Collect Sales Tax on Behalf of Pennsylvania 3rd Party Sellers*

(FAQs), TAXJAR: SALES TAX BLOG (Mar. 29, 2018), https://blog.taxjar.com/amazon-collect-pennsylvania-fba-sellers/.

Jennifer Dunn, *Breaking News! Amazon Will Now Collect 3rd Party Sales Tax in Washington*, TAXJAR: SALES TAX BLOG (Nov. 14, 2017), https://blog.taxjar.com/amazon-collect-fba-sales-tax-washington/.

Jennifer Dunn, *Sales Tax by State: Economic Nexus Laws*, TAXJAR: SALES TAX BLOG (Sept. 21, 2018), https://blog.taxjar.com/economic-nexus-laws/.

Jennifer Dunn, *What Amazon FBA Sellers Need to Know About Washington Sales Tax After January 2018*, TAXJAR: SALES TAX BLOG (Dec. 7, 2017), https://blog.taxjar.com/amazon-fba-sellers-washington-sales-tax-january-2018/.

Jennifer Dunn, *What Online Sellers Need to Know about When to Pay Income Tax*, TAXJAR: SALES TAX BLOG (Dec. 14, 2017), https://blog.taxjar.com/what-online-sellers-need-to-know-about-when-to-pay-income-tax/.

Mark Faggiano, *Do Amazon Sort Centers Create Nexus?*, TAXJAR: SALES TAX BLOG (Feb. 10, 2015), https://blog.taxjar.com/amazon-sort-centers-create-nexus/.

Mark Faggiano, Do International Sellers Have to Deal with Sales Tax in the US?, TAXJAR: SALES TAX BLOG (Apr. 10, 2018), https://blog.taxjar.com/international-sellers-deal-sales-tax-u-s/.

Mark Faggiano, *How to Register for a Sales Tax Permit in Every State*, TAXJAR: SALES TAX BLOG (Mar. 13, 2018), https://blog.taxjar.com/how-to-register-for-sales-tax-permits/.

Mark Faggiano, *Sales Tax Nexus Defined*, TAXJAR: SALES TAX BLOG (July 2, 2018), https://blog.taxjar.com/sales-tax-nexus-definition/.

Mark Faggiano, *What is Click-Through Nexus and How Does it Affect Online Sellers?*, TAXJAR: SALES TAX BLOG (Nov. 17, 2015), https://blog.taxjar.com/click-through-nexus/.

Mark Faggiano, *What's a Pass-Through Tax?*, TAXJAR: SALES TAX BLOG (May 7, 2014), https://blog.taxjar.com/sales-tax-pass-through-tax/.

Mark Faggiano, *When to Register for a Sales Tax License*, TAXJAR: SALES TAX BLOG (Aug. 30, 2017), https://blog.taxjar.com/when-register-sales-tax-license/.

Mark Faggiano, *Where to File a Sales Tax Return Even if You Didn't Collect Sales Tax*, TAXJAR: SALES TAX BLOG (Aug. 11, 2014), https://blog.taxjar.com/zero-return-sales-tax/.

Mark Faggiano, *Which States Require Sales Tax Based on Click-Through Nexus?*, TAXJAR: SALES TAX BLOG (Apr. 5, 2018), https://blog.taxjar.com/states-sales-tax-click-thru-nexus/.

Stephanie Farris, *Could You Be Held Personally Liable for Unpaid Sales Tax?*, AVALARA: TRUSTFILE (Aug. 2, 2015), https://www.avalara.com/trustfile/en/blog/could-you-be-held-personally-liable-for-unpaid-sales-tax.html.

Katherine Gustafson, *What Is Nexus and How Does It Affect Your Small Business?*, INTUIT QUICKBOOKS: QUICKBOOKS RESOURCE CTR., https://quickbooks.intuit.com/r/taxes/what-is-nexus-and-how-does-it-affect-your-small-business/ (last visited Sept. 26, 2018).

Andrew J. Haile, *Affiliate Nexus in E-Commerce*, 33 CARDOZO L. REV. 1803 (2012).

Georgene Harkness, *How to Find Where Amazon FBA Gives You Sales Tax Nexus*, TAXJAR: SALES TAX BLOG (May 8, 2018), https://blog.taxjar.com/amazon-fba-nexus/.

Chris Isidore, *Amazon to Start Collecting State Sales Taxes Everywhere*, CNNTECH (Mar. 29, 2017, 2:59 PM), https://money.cnn.com/2017/03/29/technology/amazon-sales-tax/index.html.

Anders Jorstad, *Online Merchants Guild: Shaping the Future of eCommerce*, AMAZON SELLERS LAW. (Mar. 26, 2018), https://www.amazonsellerslawyer.com/blog/online-merchants-guild-shaping-future-of-ecommerce/.

Suzanne Kearns, *Top 5 Myths About Nexus and Amazon*, AVALARA: TRUSTFILE (Feb. 15, 2017), https://www.avalara.com/trustfile/en/blog/top-5-myths-about-nexus-and-amazon.html.

Eugene Kim, *Amazon Gives in to Massachusetts Tax Officials and Agrees to Turn over Third-Party Seller Data*, CNBC (Jan. 23, 2018, 7:26 PM), https://www.cnbc.com/2018/01/23/amazon-will-turn-over-third-party-seller-tax-data-to-massachusetts.html.

Eugene Kim, *Amazon Steps into Tax Collection with Service That Could Help States Collect Billions in Lost Revenue*, CNBC (Nov. 15, 2017, 3:13 PM), https://www.cnbc.com/2017/11/15/amazon-market-place-tax-collection-comes-to-washington-in-2018.html.

Ned Lenhart, *Income Tax Nexus and Sales Tax Nexus: Is there a Difference?*, TAXJAR: SALES TAX BLOG (Sept. 2, 2015), https://blog.taxjar.com/income-tax-nexus/.

Ari Levy, *Amazon Will Start Collecting Sales Tax for Shipments to Pennsylvania as States Seek to Recoup Billions*, CNBC (Mar. 2, 2018, 6:26 PM), https://www.cnbc.com/2018/03/02/amazon-to-start-col-lecting-sales-tax-for-shipments-to-pennsylvania.html.

Marc Lifsher, Andrea Chang & Ricardo Lopez, *State to Target Web Retailers for Sales Taxes*, L.A. TIMES (Aug. 31, 2012), http://arti-cles.latimes.com/2012/aug/31/business/la-fi-0831-internet-taxes-crackdown-20120831.

Laura McCamy, *6 Steps for Dealing with a Late Sales Tax Return*, AVALARA: TRUSTFILE (Jan. 15, 2016), https://www.ava-lara.com/trustfile/en/blog/6-steps-for-dealing-with-a-late-sales-tax-return.html.

Jennifer McLoughlin, *Online Sales Tax Law Heads to South Dakota Supreme Court*, Bloomberg BNA (Apr. 6, 2017), https://www.bna.com/online-sales-tax-n57982086318/.

Jean Murray, How Businesses Pay Franchise Taxes, Balance Small Bus. (June 27, 2017), https://www.thebalancesmb.com/how-businesses-pay-franchise-taxes-398272.

Rebecca Newton-Clarke, *Nexus Considerations: Navigating the "Kill Quill" Revolt*, Thompson Reuters: Tax & Acct. Blog (Jan. 22, 2018), https://tax.thomsonreuters.com/blog/checkpoint/nexus-considerations-navigating-the-kill-quill-revolt.

Sara Schoenfield, *Much Ado About Nexus: The States Struggle to Impose Sales Tax Obligations on Out-of-State Sellers Engaged in E-Commerce*, 24 Fordham Intell. Prop., Media & Ent. L.J. 263 (2013).

Paul Shukovsky, *Amazon to Collect Third-Party Sales Tax for Washington*, Bloomberg BNA (Nov. 20, 2017), https://www.bna.com/amazon-collect-thirdparty-n73014472282/.

Spencer Soper, *Amazon's Sales Tax Fight Is Heating Up as States Crack Down*, Bloomberg (Oct. 9, 2017, 6:00 AM), https://www.bloomberg.com/news/articles/2017-10-09/amazon-s-sales-tax-fight-is-heating-up-as-states-crack-down.

David M. Steingold, *California State Business Income Tax: What Kind of Tax Will You Owe on California Business Income?*, NOLO, https://www.nolo.com/legal-encyclopedia/california-state-business-income-tax.html (last visited Sept. 26, 2018).

Laura Stevens, *Next Target for States Seeking to Collect Sales Taxes: Sellers on Amazon*, WALL STREET J. (Mar. 30, 2017, 5:30 AM), https://www.wsj.com/articles/next-target-for-states-seeking-to-collect-sales-taxes-sellers-on-amazon-1490866207/.

Jack Stewart, *"Click-Through" and "Affiliate" Nexus - What Does It All Mean?*, SCHNEIDER DOWNS: OUR THOUGHTS ON: (Apr. 15, 2013), https://www.schneiderdowns.com/our-thoughts-on/salt/click-through-affiliate-nexus.

Lauren Stinson, *Nexus Nightmares? Rest Easy with a VDA: Voluntary Disclosure Agreement*, TAXJAR: SALES TAX BLOG (June 11, 2014), https://blog.taxjar.com/voluntary-disclosure-agreement/.

Made in the USA
Monee, IL
14 July 2023

39258538R00066